PROJECT

CODE

CREATE MUSIC WITH SCRATCH

Illustrated by
Glen McBeth

Kevin Wood

Lerner Publications ◆ Minneapolis

First American edition published in 2018 by Lerner Publishing Group, Inc.

First published in Great Britain in 2017 by
The Watts Publishing Group, an imprint of Hachette Children's Group

Speech bubble designed by Freepik
Main body text set in Neo Sans Std 13/20.
Typeface provided by Monotype Typography.

Library of Congress Cataloging-in-Publication Data

The Cataloging-in-Publication Data for *Create Music with Scratch* is on
    file at the Library of Congress.
ISBN 978-1-5415-2437-8 (lib. bdg.)
ISBN 978-1-5415-2515-3 (pbk.)
ISBN 978-1-5415-2443-9 (EB pdf)

Printed in China

MIX
Paper from
responsible sources
FSC® C104740
FSC
www.fsc.org

Lerner Publications Company
A division of Lerner Publishing Group, Inc.
241 First Avenue North
Minneapolis, MN 55401 USA

For reading levels and more information, look up this title at www.lernerbooks.com.

The website addresses (URLs) included in this book were valid at the time of going to press. However, it is possible that contents or addresses may have changed since the publication of this book. No responsibility for any such changes can be accepted by either the author or the Publisher.

Using Scratch

Scratch is a programming language designed by MIT (Massachusetts Institute of Technology) that lets you create your own interactive stories, animations, games, music, and art. Rather than using a complex computer language, it uses easy-to-understand coding blocks. To get the most out of this book, you will need to be able to use a computer and you will need to load Scratch onto your computer. Always check with an adult if it is OK to download files from the Internet to your computer. Go to: **https://scratch.mit.edu**.

First, do Scratch's "Getting Started with Scratch" tutorial, found by going to "Create" on the home page, and then look in the "Tips" menu. You can also work on Scratch off-line. Scroll to the bottom of the home page and click on Offline Editor in the Support menu. Follow the instructions to install it on your computer.

CONTENTS

To load the projects that you will use in this book, go to:

www.lernerbooks.com/go/project-code-download

and select "Music." Save the folder somewhere on your computer where you will be able to find it again. You will need to open files in this folder as you go through the book.

ALL ABOUT MUSIC

>>> Music is created when sounds are arranged in an organized way. It is usually made of sounds (notes) that are pleasant to listen to. Cultures all around the world make music. Some animals, such as birds and whales, make music too! Music is made up of five main elements. If you create your own music—either by using real instruments, singing a song, or using Scratch—you will use these elements as you go along.

The elements

The five main elements of music are:

- PITCH: this is how high or low a musical note is
- MELODY: this is the tune or pattern the notes make as they are played
- HARMONY: this is when three or more notes are played at the same time. Together they form a **chord**.
  - RHYTHM: this is how sounds (and silences) in music are arranged as they move forward in time. Clapping your hands in time to a beat is a rhythm and the speed of that rhythm is called the **tempo**.
  - TONE: this is the particular sound each instrument makes. A piano and a trumpet can play the same note at the same pitch, but they both sound very different.

Starting from Scratch

Writing music and writing computer **code** have a lot in common. Computer code is a set of instructions that tell a computer what to do. Written music is a set of instructions that tell a musician what to do.

Scratch has all kinds of ways to make great music. You can write code with sounds from the Scratch Sound Library. Open Scratch and click on the "Sounds" tab. Then click on the speaker symbol to get to the Sound Library. You'll see a list of all the different noises you can use.

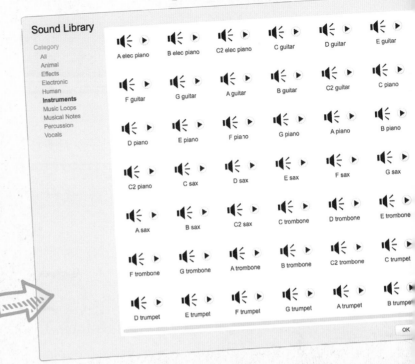

Click on the play button (▶) of some of the sounds to hear them in action.

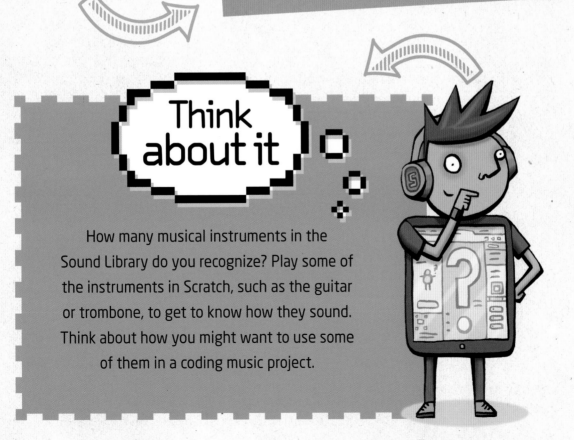

Think about it

How many musical instruments in the Sound Library do you recognize? Play some of the instruments in Scratch, such as the guitar or trombone, to get to know how they sound. Think about how you might want to use some of them in a coding music project.

MAKING MUSIC

Until the late 1980s, most early computers could only make one sound—a beep! It was hard to make music on these early computers.

In some of the first computer games, the beep was **programmed** to change in length and pitch, creating a simple tune. Today's computers have sound cards. A sound card allows a computer to create and record high-quality and more complicated sounds. Microphones or speakers can be plugged into the computer too, to record or play back sound.

What is sound?

Sounds are made of **pressure waves** that travel in straight lines. We hear sounds when the waves **vibrate** our **eardrums**. The vibrations are turned into electrical signals that our brains understand as sound. Different sounds have different-sized waves.

Loud sounds create big sound waves.

Quiet sounds create small sound waves.

Think about it

What sort of waves do you think high sounds and low sounds make? Hint: a high sound vibrates faster than a low sound.

(answer on page 32)

Try it

Computer **programs** create wave shapes to make sounds. Sometimes a computer uses **samples** of real instruments to make its musical sounds. You can see the sound waves of the Sound Library samples in Scratch. Double-click on the Hip Hop sample. Then click the play button. You'll hear the sound and see a blue line moving along the sound wave as the sample plays.

MP3

All that sound wave information means music **files** are often very large. Files can be made smaller by saving them in an **MP3 format**. This format gets rid of any extra sounds on the files that the human ear can't actually hear. Smaller files mean that songs in MP3 format can be downloaded more quickly, and you can store more of them on your computer or smartphone.

7

DIFFERENT NOTES

Usually music is written on a **stave**. A stave is a set of five horizontal lines and four spaces. Each line or space represents a particular note. When music is written on a stave, it looks like the picture below. You can play with an animation of how a stave works if you load project "Staff.sb2."

Musical magic

Make the wizard **sprite** play the notes by clicking the green flag, then pressing the up and down arrows on your keyboard or by clicking on a note's letter on the right of the screen. If you click on each sprite you can see the code used to create it. It is a little complicated, but there is no need to understand it at the moment—just have fun with it!

See if you can make the wizard play the C Major **scale**, which is pictured below.

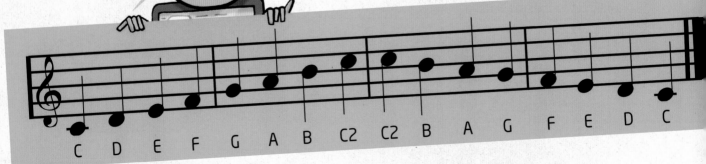

Create a tune

In Scratch, the notes in the Sound Library have eight different pitches. C is the lowest and C2 is the highest (see page 8). You don't actually need to know how to read or write music to make tunes in Scratch.

Click on the "Musical Notes" category in the Sound Library's left-hand menu. Pick an instrument and play the notes from C to C2. Then see if you can make up a tune using these eight notes. Write down the names of your notes in the order you played them if you want to use this tune when you write your own code.

My tune
A, C2, B, G, A

Think about it

A music scale always starts and finishes with the same note. The C Major scale begins and ends with a C—CDEFGABC, using eight notes. These eight notes are known as an octave. The word octave comes from the **Latin** word *octavus*, which means eighth. Can you think of any other words that start with "oct?"

(answers on page 32)

USER INTERACTION

A user is the person using a computer program. The code written for that program usually responds to a user's actions. For example, in the "Staff.sb2" project on page 8, you (the user) made the wizard sprite move and the notes play by pressing the keyboard's arrow keys or by clicking on a letter. This is called user interaction.

When we write code, we can get the user to interact with the program in lots of different ways. For example, we can:

- ask the user to type the answer to a question, using the keyboard
- ask the user to click on an object or to start some music playing
- display an image and wait for the user to press a key.

When they do, the program might respond with a sound, an image, or an **animation**, depending on which key was pressed.

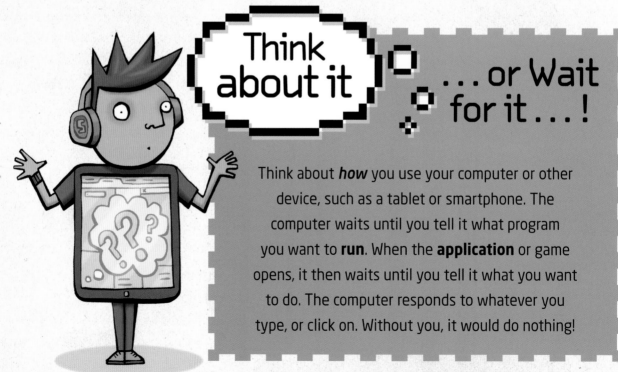

Think about it
...or Wait for it...!

Think about **how** you use your computer or other device, such as a tablet or smartphone. The computer waits until you tell it what program you want to **run**. When the **application** or game opens, it then waits until you tell it what you want to do. The computer responds to whatever you type, or click on. Without you, it would do nothing!

In a way, a musical instrument is a bit like a computer. A piano is a very complicated instrument that can make all kinds of beautiful music. But it will sit there in silence without user interaction!

AHA!

Coding unplugged

Computers can be annoying if their user interaction is confusing!
For example, to shut down some computers, users have to press the "Start" button. That's confusing! Try this user interaction test on a friend to see how confusing getting two sets of information can be.

You will need: a friend, three pens (red, green, and blue), and three pieces of paper.

1 Write the word "red" in blue pen on the first piece of paper.
Write the word "green" in red pen on the second piece of paper.
Write the word "blue" in green pen on the third piece of paper.

2 Quickly flash up the pieces of paper and ask your friend to say what color they see. It's amazing how hard this can be. It's confusing because the brain gets two sets of information—the word and the color—at the same time.

RED   GREEN   BLUE

People who create code need to understand how users think. This helps them to design easy-to-use programs.

RHYTHM

>>> A beat is a steady pulse, such as a heartbeat. In music, beats are usually played on drums. You make a rhythm by playing a pattern of notes over the background of that steady beat. >>>

Coding unplugged

Use two wooden spoons as drumsticks. Use a book and a metal pan lid as instruments. See if you can follow these instructions and drum this simple rhythm with your left hand while your right hand plays the beat. The rhythm repeats itself every four beats.

You will need: a book, a metal pan lid, and two wooden spoons.

Right hand (beat)

hit book (one beat)

hit book (one beat)

hit book (one beat)

hit book (one beat)

. . . and repeat

Left hand (rhythm)

do nothing (one beat)

do nothing (one beat)

do nothing (one beat)

hit pan lid (one beat)

. . . and repeat

This takes a bit of practice, but once you've mastered it, try speeding it up and slowing it down to change the tempo of the beat.

Creating a rhythm on Scratch

Load the project called "Rapper.sb2." It has a rapper sprite and a background from the Scratch Backdrop Library. Now try some user interaction.

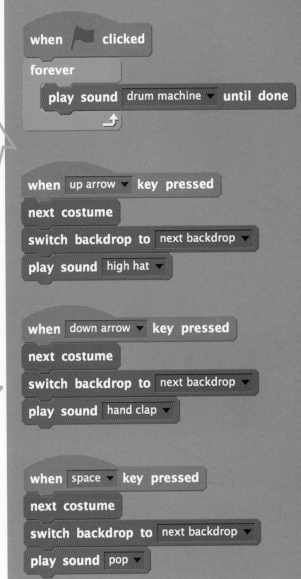

1 Click the green flag to start the beat.

2 Press the up arrow key on your keyboard to make the rapper change position (change costume), change the background, and make the "high-hat" sound.

3 Press the down arrow on your keyboard to make the rapper change costume, change the background, and make the "hand clap" sound.

4 Press the space bar to make the rapper change position, change the background, and make the "pop" sound.

How the code works

These codes use three blocks each and need user interaction (see pages 10-11) to make them run. The first block of code waits for the user to press a key. When the key is pressed the other three blocks spring into action.

The second block tells the sprite to change to the "next costume" so it looks like he is dancing. The third block changes the backdrop. The fourth block plays a sound. To change the sounds, click on the drop-down menu on the "play sound" block of code and select a new sound.

Try it

Try tapping the keys in a rhythm to get the rapper to dance and play sounds in time to the beat. Can you make up a sequence that you like?

PROJECT PAGE:
PLAYING A SIMPLE TUNE

In Scratch we can play simple tunes by building up blocks of code. Load the project "RR1.sb2" and click on the flag. The tune plays and an animation bounces a ball along the words.

when 🏁 clicked

The first part of the code tells the computer to wait until the green flag is clicked. If you click it, the code below it will run.

The instrument (no. 1) is a piano, and the tempo is set to 180 bpm (beats per minute). Try changing the tempo and run the code again. What do you notice?

set instrument to **1▾**
set tempo to **180** bpm

Numbered notes

In Scratch, every note has a number. The first note is low C (number 48 in Scratch). It is played for one-and-a-half beats. You can see the numbers each note is given by clicking on the play note drop-down menu and hovering your pointer over the pop-up keyboard.

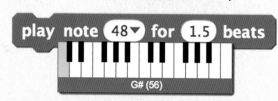

play note **48▾** for **1.5** beats

G# (56)

AHA!

The bigger the number you set as the beat for each note, the longer that note will play for. A beat of 2 will play for twice as long as a beat of 1.

Playing the tune as a round

If you know this tune then you will know that it is usually played as a round. A round is a simple song that overlaps as it repeats itself. To hear the round being played, load project "RR2.sb2" and click the green flag.

Have a rest

The two sets of code look almost the same. The difference is that the set on the right has one extra line of code, a rest.

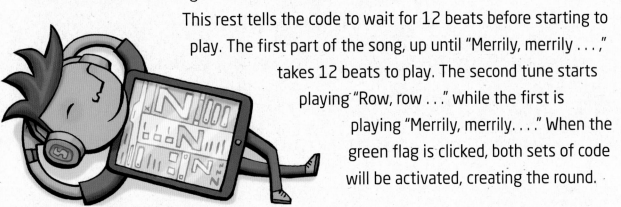

This rest tells the code to wait for 12 beats before starting to play. The first part of the song, up until "Merrily, merrily . . . ," takes 12 beats to play. The second tune starts playing "Row, row . . ." while the first is playing "Merrily, merrily. . . ." When the green flag is clicked, both sets of code will be activated, creating the round.

Animate it

To make your music even more fun in Scratch, you can add your own animation. The rowing dog for this piece of music was made by drawing two dog sprites and swapping between them. Click on the dog sprite, then on "Costumes" to see the two costume drawings.

The backdrop was made by altering the "underwater3" backdrop in the Backdrop Library. To change a backdrop, select one and then click on the "Backdrops" tab at the top to see the range of tools available to alter it.

REPETITION

Music has a handy shortcut for repeating sections. Instead of writing out the instructions over and over, **composers** use a repeat symbol.

The two bracket shapes mark where you start and end the section to be repeated. You can repeat the section once, a number of times, or until the performer decides to stop.

Loops

Computer code can do the same thing. Programmers use **loops** to tell the computer to repeat a set of instructions. In Scratch, you can create a loop to:

- repeat the code forever
- repeat the code a number of times
- repeat the code until something else happens

To do this in Scratch, you use the REPEAT, FOREVER, or REPEAT UNTIL loop blocks, which you can find in the "Control" menu.

The animation of the rowing dog uses a repeat loop to change from one costume to the next, 48 times, as she moves across the screen.

```
when [flag] clicked
show
go to x: -250 y: -16
repeat 48
    set y to -16
    change x by 11
    next costume
    wait 0.25 secs
hide
```

Using loops makes code shorter and easier to read, spot mistakes, and make changes to it.

Think about it

What kind of loop do you think you would use if you wanted the dog to sit in the boat and row all the way through the song? A forever loop or a repeat loop?

(answer on page 32)

Music loops

Composers often use a quick way of writing looping instructions. Composers name parts of the music, such as "verse" or "chorus." Once the musicians know what notes or other instructions each section contains, the composer can simply write "verse" or "chorus," and the musicians will know what to play.

Coding does a similar thing. A programmer can create a subroutine, and then just type in the name of that subroutine, rather than the whole set of instructions.

Subroutines

Subroutines make code even easier to read, as we can name them whatever we want. Scratch allows you to create a new block of code and give it a name. You can then use this named subroutine again and again, rather than building long and complicated blocks of code every time you want to repeat something.

LOOPS AND SUBROUTINES

Load project "RR3.sb2" and click the green flag. The tune plays and the dog rows, just as before. Now look at the code. What differences can you see?

The difference is that the code looks much shorter and simpler, because we have used repeat loops and subroutines.

define Play

Making a subroutine

when ⚑ clicked

Play

Click on the piano sprite and look at the script for the piano. You can see that we have created a new subroutine block called "Play." Subroutines are made in the "More Blocks" section. We clicked "Make a Block," called it "Play," and then added all the code for the music to the block. When we want to use this subroutine, we now only need to select the Play block, because this one block contains all of the code we need to play the music.

Next, load project "RR4.sb2" and click the green flag. The round now plays four times.

18

Using repeat loops

Look at the script for the piano and you will see that a repeat loop has been added to the Play subroutine. This tells the computer to repeat the code inside the block twice.

Now each time we use "Play" it will play all of the notes twice. To play four rounds we use the block twice—the second time with the added block of code telling it to wait for 12 beats.

Think about it

Try changing the number of times the loop repeats. How do you think this will affect what the song will sound like?

Coding unplugged

Try making up a simple dance to go with the music. You could include a rowing action, followed by making a wave motion with your arms, followed by a swaying laugh during the "merrily" part. If you were going to draw your routine to teach it to other people, which parts of your dance would be best written as a loop?

PROJECT PAGE:
MULTITASKING

>>> Music is often more than one instrument playing at a time. Think about your favorite band or piece of music. How many instruments and singers are there making music at the same time? Together they create one piece of music.

Open project "ode.sb2" to see how multitasking is used to play "Ode to Burt in C." You will see four **cellos** on a stage. Clicking on each cello makes it play its individual part. Clicking on the green flag makes all four play at once.

1. Load project "Keyboard 1.sb2." First, click on the square button in the top left-hand corner of the screen. This makes the piano fill your screen. It also stops you from accidentally moving the keys when you play them. (Click the same button again when you are finished to get back to the main Scratch screen.)

2. Click on the black and white keys to play the piano.

3 The keyboard is made by creating a sprite for each key. There are 15 white key sprites and 10 black key sprites. A multitasking code runs when each sprite is clicked.

4 The multitasking code for each white key does three things at the same time, then two more things at the same time, from just one user interaction:
- the costume is changed to yellow, to show the key being pressed
- the backdrop changes, to show the name of the note in lights on the side of a building
- the note itself is played for half a beat.

Then . . .
- the costume is changed back to white
- the backdrop is changed to the original backdrop.

5 When one of the black keys is pressed, the multitasking code changes the costume to yellow to show the key being pressed, the note is played for half a beat, and then the costume is changed back to black.

PROJECT PAGE:
SENDING MESSAGES

There is another way to multitask in your code. If we make a small change to the code on pages 20–21, we can get one sprite to control another sprite by sending it a message. First we need to write the code for the message, then we need the code to **broadcast** the message.

Load project "Keyboard 2.sb2." The keyboard plays in the same way as the previous project, but if you look at the script for any of the keys, you will see a change to the code.

Message received, loud and clear!

When a key sprite is clicked, instead of simply running the code as before, it now sends a message. In this case the message is "48," as this is the number of the note the key will play.

The next section of code looks for the message it needs to receive to run the rest of the code. When message "48" is received, it plays the note. Each key in this project is waiting for a different message to be broadcast.

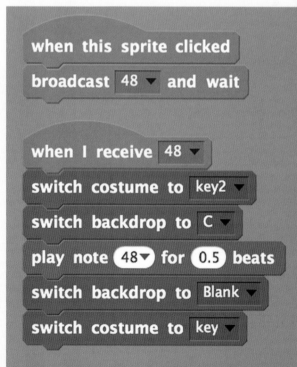

Sequences

A **sequence** is a series of instructions. Click on the aircraft in the top right-hand corner of the screen. When that sprite is clicked, we send a sequence of broadcasts to the keys numbered from 48 to 72. Broadcasts allow one sprite to talk to another.

Each key sprite is waiting for a message. Key 48 is waiting for a message called 48. When it receives the message, it plays its note. You can change the order of the broadcast sequence by changing the number on each block of code. Try it!

The code on the right is very long! In project "Keyboard 3.sb2" we have made the long bit of code shorter using a repeat loop. We tell the code to add 1 to the note's number using the "change note by" block to get to the next number. For example:

48 + 1 = 4

AHA!

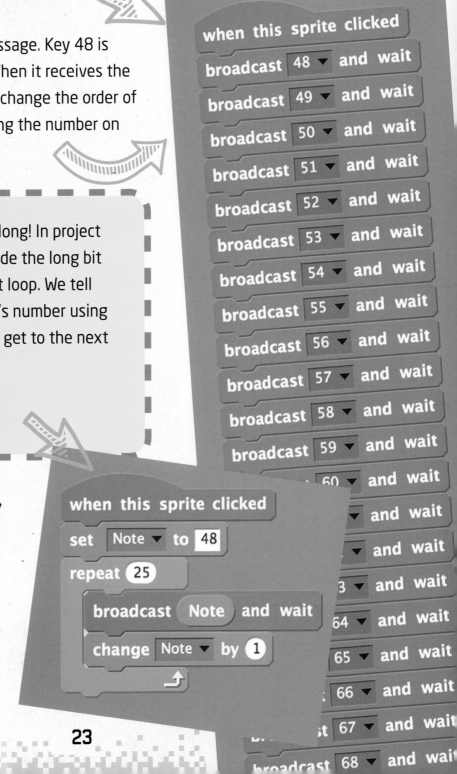

```
when this sprite clicked
broadcast  48 ▼  and wait
broadcast  49 ▼  and wait
broadcast  50 ▼  and wait
broadcast  51 ▼  and wait
broadcast  52 ▼  and wait
broadcast  53 ▼  and wait
broadcast  54 ▼  and wait
broadcast  55 ▼  and wait
broadcast  56 ▼  and wait
broadcast  57 ▼  and wait
broadcast  58 ▼  and wait
broadcast  59 ▼  and wait
          60 ▼  and wait
             ▼  and wait
             ▼  and wait
          3 ▼  and wait
          64 ▼  and wait
          65 ▼  and wait
          66 ▼  and wait
          67 ▼  and wait
broadcast  68 ▼  and wai
```

```
when this sprite clicked
set  Note ▼  to  48
repeat  25
    broadcast  Note  and wait
    change  Note ▼  by  1
```

PROJECT PAGE:
COMPOSING WITH CHORDS

>>> A chord is three or more musical notes played at the same time. They are usually played on instruments, such as a guitar or a piano. You can program Scratch to play a chord by asking it to play several sounds at once.

Now you try it!

1 Open a new Scratch project. Choose a guitar or piano from the music-themed sprites menu.

2 To create your script, first go to "Events" and drag a "When space key pressed" block over to the blank space on the right. If you want to, you can change the space key to any key from the menu.

3 Go to "Sound" and choose three "play sound" blocks and place them under your Events block.

when space ▼ key pressed
play sound C2 guitar ▼
play sound C2 guitar ▼
play sound C2 guitar ▼

4 Next, choose three notes from C to C2 from the drop-down menu to make your chord. Chords are made up of several different notes that sound good when played together. You can make as many chords as you like, but you'll need to create a separate block of code for each chord.

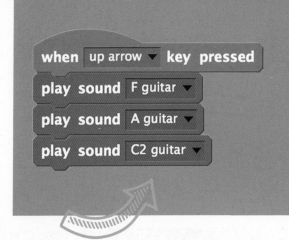

Try it

Want some inspiration? Open project "chords.sb2." The first four chords are operated with the arrow keys. There is also a separated chord, operated by the space key. This was created by using "play sound until done" blocks. Unlike the "play sound" blocks, this plays one note at a time. It won't play the next note until the first one has finished playing.

Can you play a tune using the arrow keys? Perhaps finish your tune by pressing the space key and playing the separated chord. Have fun changing the notes and the instruments. Maybe create some background animation too.

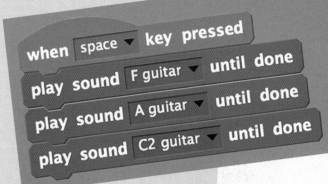

Think about it

Can you think of another way to make the instruments play? Try clicking on the picture of the guitar. Try clicking the keyboard too. Or you can program the sprites to play your tune by adding in broadcast sequence blocks (see pages 22-23).

PROJECT PAGE:
SURPRISE YOURSELF!

>>> Computers can be programmed to produce all kinds of sounds. Another great thing about computers is that they can also give you the unexpected. Try this fun project and create a surprise tune every time!

For this project you will use an operator. Operators control how a computer uses **data** and handles sequences of things. In this Scratch project, a "pick random" operator block makes a decision about which sound will play each time you hit a key. It makes the choice, not you.

1 Open a new Scratch project. Choose an instrument from the music-themed sprites. Look at the sounds that your instrument can play by clicking on the "Sounds" tab. Play each sound by selecting it and clicking the play button.

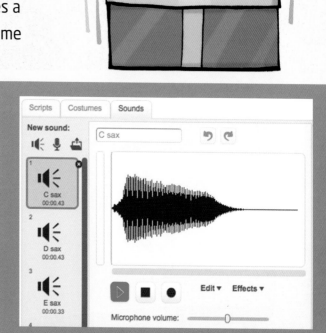

2 Next, copy the code on the right. Drag your code blocks into place on the right-hand side of your screen.

```
when  right arrow ▼  key  pressed
play sound  pick random ① to ⑧
change color ▼ effect by ㉕
```

3 Press the right arrow on your keyboard to play a random sound. Create a "tune" by hitting the arrow key again and again. The computer will pick the sounds and you will get a weird-sounding tune!

To add the green operator section, pick it up and hover it over the drop-down box in the "play sound" code block until you see the drop-down glow white. Then drop the operator block into place. Change the number values to match the number of sounds your instrument makes.

Random jazz

Open the Scratch project named "Jazz.sb2" and play a tune using the left and right arrow keys at the same time. You'll never get the same tune twice!

You can have even more fun with this project by changing the background or by adding another instrument sprite. Make sure you use a different key to operate the new sprite when you write its code.

WHAT'S A BUG?

>>> It would be great to think that every time we wrote some code, it did exactly what we wanted, in exactly the way we intended, the very first time. This is very rare, though. >>>

In reality we almost always get something wrong, or the code doesn't do exactly what we expected. This isn't always the programmer's fault. Sometimes the program that you use to write your code has a problem, which means that it produces the wrong code for you.

When your code has a problem, we say that it has a "bug." Looking carefully at the code to see what is causing the bug and then fixing it is called "debugging."

Testing

Once you have written your code you need to test it thoroughly. Does it do what you wanted? Does it do everything that you wanted? What if the user does something unexpected? Does your code then have a problem, or does it still work OK?

Debugging

If something isn't right, look through your code very carefully to see where you went wrong. Be careful that any changes do not cause another bug! Once you have fixed the bug you need to test your code thoroughly again.

Debugging is an **iterative** process. That is, you need to keep doing it until everything works as it should. The cycle is to test–repair–test. Only when the final test shows no bugs at all can we say that our code is finished.

Think about it

In large, complicated computer programs, some bugs are not noticed for a long time. That is why programs are always updated with new versions, as bugs are being fixed. Even the best programmers accidentally create bugs. Don't be put off if your code goes wrong, just test–repair–test!

When you played with these music projects, did anything go wrong? Did everything always do what you expected or did you have to fix some bugs?

GLOSSARY

animation An animated cartoon.

application A computer program that performs a major task.

broadcast The act of sending a message.

cello A large musical instrument of the violin family.

chord A group of three or more tones sounded together to form harmony.

code A set of instructions for a computer.

composer A person who writes music.

data Information for use in a computer.

eardrum The thin membrane that separates the outer and middle ear.

files Collections of data.

format The general organization or arrangement of something.

high-hat A pair of foot-operated cymbals forming part of a drum kit (also hi-hat).

iterative When a series of operations is repeated a number of times.

Latin The language of ancient Rome.

loops Series of instructions that are repeated until a requirement for ending is met, but may loop infinitely.

MP3 A means of compressing music into a very small file.

pressure wave A sound wave.

programmed Provided a program.

programs Step-by-step instructions that tell a computer to do something with data.

run To operate.

sample A part of a whole.

scale A series of tones going up or down in pitch with each tone having a fixed relationship to those above and below it.

sequence The order in which things are or should be connected.

sprite A simple, two-dimensional bitmap character that can be moved around within a larger scene.

stave The five horizontal lines and the spaces between them on which music is written (also staff).

tempo The speed at which a musical piece is to be played or sung.

vibrate A quivering effect.

MORE INFORMATION

BOOKS

Anniss, Matt. *Create Your Own Music (Media Genius)*. Oxford: Raintree, 2016.

Gifford, Clive. *Get Ahead in Computing: Computing and Coding in the Real World.* London: Wayland, 2017.

Wainewright, Max. *Generation Code: I'm an Advanced Scratch Coder.* London: Wayland, 2017.

WEBSITES

MIT's Scratch website, where you can download the program for free

https://scratch.mit.edu/about/

VISIT

The **Computer History Museum,** Mountain View, California, has activities and events for families exploring computer history. **The GRAMMY Museum,** Los Angeles, California, frequently hosts music production classes for kids. Check out these museums or look for similar programs in your area.

INDEX

ANSWERS

page 7   High sounds make waves that are close together. Low sounds make waves that are far apart. Think of a high sound wave as a tightly coiled spring and a low sound wave as a spring that has been stretched.

page 9   Here are three words that start with "oct":
- An **octopus** is an eight-legged sea creature.
- An **octogon** is an eight-sided shape.
- **October** is the *tenth* month of the year, but in the ancient Roman calendar it was the eighth month of the year.

page 17   You would use a forever loop to make the dog row—forever.